This book belongs to:

_____

_____

_____

Design & Layout:
Beth Merck, Clare Sosso

Photography:
Jon Combs

Merck Family's
Old World Christmas®
P.O. Box 8000
Spokane, WA 99203

Printed in U.S.A.
Fifth Edition

Christmas Ornament Legends

A Collection of Stories, Traditions, and Folklore from

Old World Christmas®

This book is dedicated to our children,
Jonathan and Katherine. May they preserve these legends
and keep the joy of Christmas in their hearts.

An Heirloom is Born — The Making of a Glass Ornament.

The natural beauty of a glass ornament embodies the laborious process of its creation. The steps involved in creating tomorrow's glass heirlooms are indeed numerous but are exactly as they were years ago. These skills were perfected by gifted German artisans and passed down from generation to generation in the authentic tradition of creating genuine, cherished Christmas heirlooms.

Nestled deep in the Franconian mountains of Northern Bavaria is the birthplace of the glass Christmas ornament. At Inge-Glas™, founded by the direct descendants of the original glassblowers of Lauscha, the time-honored art of German glassblowing endures to this day. This family of gifted artisans represents a living legacy to the exceptional talent and dedication needed to create tomorrow's heirlooms today.

Each glassblower begins with a "blank", a small hollow ball of glass with a long stem. Heated over a flame until it is red hot, the blank is set into the bottom half of a porcelain mold and then covered with the top half. The glassblower then blows in the stem until the molten glass conforms to the shape of the mold. He then removes the ornament, reheats it a second time and gives the stem one final puff. This extra step tempers the orna-ment, thereby preventing stress cracks.

Once the orna-ment has cooled, it is silvered. A mixture of silver nitrate, ammonia and distilled water is poured into the ornament along with a few drops of a combination of saltpeter, sugar and more distilled water. The ornament is then dipped into a hot water bath where the muddy-brown mixture magically turns into a glistening silver color. When rinsed, the ornament is placed upside down on a nail and set in a drying oven.

After completely drying, the silvered ornament is taken to the artist's table for painting. Applying each color individually is a separate process and the ornament is repeatedly set aside to dry before the next color may be added. This can involve up to thirty applications and requires much skill on the part of the artisan to ensure exacting detail and that one color does not overlap another.

Glitter is then applied to the ornament to add sparkling highlights, the stem is broken off, and the trademark star cap of quality is put into place. An heirloom is born and the radiant new ornament takes its prop-er place on the Christmas tree to offer its exquisite beauty to Christmas celebrations for generations to come.

Old World Christmas®

Inge-Glas was first founded in 1953, by Heinz Müller-Blech, a thirteenth generation glassblower and direct descendant of renowned Lauscha glassblower Christoph Müller. Heinz, together with his new bride Inge, continued their glassblowing heritage when they started producing ornaments in a small workshop in their home on the shore of a peaceful lake in a secluded German village. Their dedication to quality and to their craft shone in every gleaming treasure they created. Their early specialty was birds with gossamer wings and tails of spun glass. Their fine skills and pride in craftsmanship, along with many cherished antique molds, have been passed on to a fourteenth generation, Heinz and Inge's son Klaus. Klaus and his wife Birgit, daughter of master German glassblower Erwin Eichhorn, now manage the family business. This family-owned firm has become one of the largest producers of genuine, hand-crafted, traditional glass ornaments in the world.

The trademark star cap, the star of quality, is your assurance of genuine, heirloom-quality glass ornaments made in Germany by Inge-Glas. Produced in limited quantities and exclusively imported by Old World Christmas, these dazzling, delicate and affordable collectibles are treasures you and your family are sure to enjoy as part of your Christmas memories and traditions.

Bring the joy and magic of a traditional, old-fashioned Christmas to your home with authentic figural glass ornaments from Old World Christmas.

Ornament Legends

Old World Christmas®

The Story of a Legend

Storytelling has long been an integral part of German culture. German people have always been fond of tradition and are very protective of their heritage, particularly surrounding the celebration of Christmas. Often credited with introducing the Christmas tree to the world, the German people's stories and holiday customs are the foundation of the legends that accompany many Old World Christmas ornaments.

Centuries ago, in tiny villages throughout the German countryside, parents amused their children on cold wintry nights with the telling of magical stories and fairy tales. These stories, often repeated many times over the years, became an inherent part of the children's lives and memories. As they grew, they too passed these stories on to their own children, creating a legacy of cultural pride and family traditions. As dialects and accents varied from village to village, so did traditional family legends, yet each tale was treasured by the family who told it.

Old World Christmas first introduced Christmas ornament legends to American collectors with the whimsical story of the pickle ornament. The tradition of hiding a pickle ornament in the tree was first discovered by Tim and Beth Merck of Old World Christmas while visiting a small hamlet in Germany. The contagious merriment and delight of the old woman telling the story was a feeling Tim and Beth wanted to share with families in the United States. Additional visits to other villages and conversations with German families eager to share their fond Christmas memories uncovered a wealth of Christmas traditions, ready to be shared with the world.

Old World Christmas takes great pleasure in providing an opportunity for today's collectors to share the same magical legends with their friends and families during the holidays through this collection of Christmas ornament traditions.

Old World Christmas®

Bells rang throughout the world when Christ was born, according to early legend. Traditionally, bells have been used throughout Europe and America to ring in the Christmas season. The ringing of bells during the holiday season provides a joyful accompaniment to the festive singing of favorite carols. Bells have come to represent a vital part of Christmas celebrations as church bells and sleigh bells brighten winter days with their joyous tinkle. Bell ornaments symbolize the joy and merriment of the Christmas holidays, and are a welcome addition to Christmas traditions.

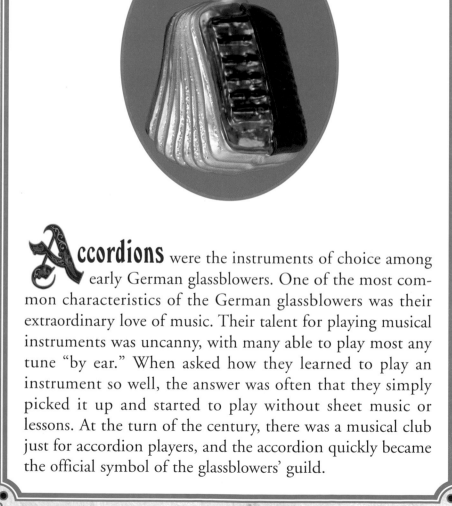

Accordions were the instruments of choice among early German glassblowers. One of the most common characteristics of the German glassblowers was their extraordinary love of music. Their talent for playing musical instruments was uncanny, with many able to play most any tune "by ear." When asked how they learned to play an instrument so well, the answer was often that they simply picked it up and started to play without sheet music or lessons. At the turn of the century, there was a musical club just for accordion players, and the accordion quickly became the official symbol of the glassblowers' guild.

offee Pots are symbolic of hospitality. In Germany, as in America, it is customary to bring a gift of thanks to the hosts whenever entering their home in appreciation of their invitation. As common household items were duplicated as whimsical tree decorations made by German glassblowers, the glass Coffee Pot Christmas tree ornament delighted many homemakers. A popular gift and party favor, this traditional ornament often was given to commemorate an anniversary, cheer a new home or to accompany an actual coffee pot as a gift.

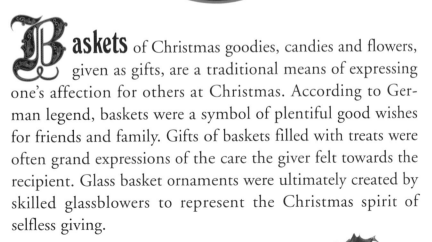

Baskets of Christmas goodies, candies and flowers, given as gifts, are a traditional means of expressing one's affection for others at Christmas. According to German legend, baskets were a symbol of plentiful good wishes for friends and family. Gifts of baskets filled with treats were often grand expressions of the care the giver felt towards the recipient. Glass basket ornaments were ultimately created by skilled glassblowers to represent the Christmas spirit of selfless giving.

Old World Christmas®

Rabbits are very shy and frail animals by nature. Having no natural means of protecting itself, the rabbit is therefore dependent on the kindness of man and other animals for its survival. In religious tales the rabbit came to symbolize man and his placement of hope and faith in Christ for protection. As a result, German folklore instructed children to prepare nests for rabbits to offer them shelter. At Christmas time the rabbit represents the renewal of this faith in others to provide guidance, protection, and kindness.

Christmas Carp has long been festive fare for the holidays in Germany, and this tradition is observed in many central European homes to this day. Carefully prepared during the day, this delicate fish was grandly presented to family and friends on Christmas often elaborately garnished with sprigs of holly, citrus slices, and berries. German glassblowers created many fish ornaments over the years, primarily as the symbolic Christian image originated by the ancient Greeks. The creation of the Christmas Carp ornament was in commemoration of the traditional German Christmas feast.

Old World Christmas®

Weather Frogs were traditional German weather forecasters! Many families in Germany, especially those living on farms, often used a large canning jar to create a frog's aquarium and equipped it with a small ladder. When the weather was about to improve, the frog could be seen climbing his ladder to enjoy the sunshine. When it was humid or was going to rain, he descended the ladder and jumped back into the water. The clever frog unknowingly provided German farmers a "foolproof" means of forecasting the weather!

Birds are considered a universal symbol of happiness and joy and are regarded by many to be a necessity on the Christmas tree. Glassblowers would often carefully capture wild birds in autumn to keep in cages in their workshops and to shelter them during the winter months. The sound of the gas flame from the Bunsen burners used to make glass ornaments would prompt the birds to sing throughout the day, thereby entertaining the entire family. Because bird ornaments were difficult to create, few glassblowing families in Germany specialized in the making of these special pieces.

Many collectors remember the lovely glass bird ornaments delicately perched on their grandmother's tree, which is one reason birds have continued to be among the most coveted of glass ornaments. Even today, birds represent messengers of love and the harbingers of good things to come.

Old World Christmas®

Bird's nest ornaments are symbols of good luck. Legend has it that prosperity will come to any home that finds a bird's nest nestled among the branches of the family's Christmas tree. As a promise of this good fortune, glassblowers produced exquisite ornaments replicating this fortuitous symbol. Considered synonymous with home, happiness and joy, birds and their nests can be found on every traditional German Christmas tree.

Cottages, nestled in quaint little villages in the mountains and forests of Germany, represent the heritage and culture of the glassblowers. The unique architecture of each village was a source of great pride as cottage styles often varied greatly. Glassblowers frequently created images that reflected their day-to-day lives. Therefore Cottage ornaments were proudly styled after the humble homes in which the artisans lived and worked, as well as after the fanciful gingerbread houses families made during the Christmas season.

Mushrooms have long been good luck symbols in the German culture. Found in the beautiful forests of Europe, mushrooms are closely associated with nature and the beauty and mystery of the forest. Finding a mushroom in the woods was like finding a lucky penny - good fortune was just around the corner! Additionally, discovering a double mushroom was considered to be even more serendipitous. It is said that every Christmas tree in Germany proudly displays at least one Mushroom ornament in honor of the people's reverence for nature and hopes for good luck in the coming year.

Red Riding Hood represents family values and the doctrine that children should obey their parents and remain wary of strangers. The German fable of Little Red Riding Hood was first recorded by Jakob and Wilhelm Grimm, widely known as the Brothers Grimm. According to the tale, Little Red Riding Hood always wore a red velvet hood sewn by her grandmother when she went outside. On an errand for her mother, Little Red Riding Hood disobeyed her mother and left the main path she was to follow. The big bad wolf swiftly spotted the errant girl and led Little Red Riding Hood astray. Just as she was about to be swallowed by the wolf, she was rescued by a brave hunter passing by in the forest. To remind children of this beloved fairy tale, glassblowers created the popular Red Riding Hood glass ornament.

Ladybugs, or ladybug beetles, received their name centuries ago in Europe. Farmers were experiencing serious problems with aphids which were sucking the juices from their grape vines. The farmers prayed to the Virgin Mary for help, and soon thousands of little red beetles appeared and ate the aphids. The farmers truly believed their prayers had been answered and named the helpful beetles in honor of Mary, who was also known as "Our Lady." In Germany, ladybugs are called Marienkäfer, Marien for Mary and Käfer for beetle. Due to its helpful nature, the ladybug is considered a good luck symbol in Germany.

Old World Christmas®

Chimney Sweeps, dressed in the traditional garb of their profession, are an enchanting sight for all to see. German folklore tells us that to be touched by a chimney sweep will bring you good luck. To most, receiving a lingering black sooty smudge is a small price to pay for a bit of his good fortune. The glass Chimney Sweep ornament brings providence and fortune to those who hang it on their Christmas tree during the holidays.

26

Star ornaments originated as a symbol of guidance and faith, representing the Star of Bethlehem which led the Magi to the manger where Christ was born. Brilliant stars are frequently placed above a crèche or atop the Christmas tree as part of cherished family traditions. German glassblowers have created star ornaments for centuries as dazzling reminders of the significant role stars have played in Christmas traditions, representing the true magic of the heavens.

Old World Christmas®

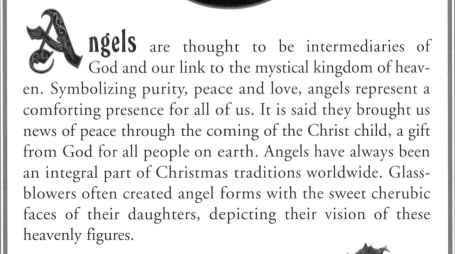

Angels are thought to be intermediaries of God and our link to the mystical kingdom of heaven. Symbolizing purity, peace and love, angels represent a comforting presence for all of us. It is said they brought us news of peace through the coming of the Christ child, a gift from God for all people on earth. Angels have always been an integral part of Christmas traditions worldwide. Glassblowers often created angel forms with the sweet cherubic faces of their daughters, depicting their vision of these heavenly figures.

Devils with red faces, horns and tails often played a significant role in early German Christmas celebrations. Paradise plays performed during the holiday season in medieval times depicted life and death, the Garden of Eden, and good and evil. Devil heads were an important part of early Christian celebrations of Christmas to remind revelers of the consequences of living an unholy life. In some parts of Germany and Austria, St. Nicholas characters were accompanied by a figure called Krampus. Krampus looked very much like the devil and his purpose was to punish girls and boys who had misbehaved during the year. This ornament is symbolic of the devil figure common to early Christmas festivals, and the antique mold for the Devil Head ornament is believed to be one of the earliest molds made.

Old World Christmas®

Clowns represent the merry, jesting nature of the German people. The 500,000 Clown ornament was inspired by the runaway inflation in Germany following World War I and the significant loss of value of the German currency, the mark. Satirists of the time said that 500,000 German marks were needed to buy a loaf of bread! The 500,000 Clown ornament was created to denote this difficult time in German history. As bakers throughout the region had their own insignia, glassblowers added a gold medallion on the front of the ornament to reflect the baker's emblem.

Liberty Bell ornaments are the most patriotic of Christmas decorations. Patriotic ornaments exquisitely painted in red, white and blue, were among the most popular glass tree decorations in America at the turn of the century. Patriotic bells symbolized the joyful celebration of the end of World War I. German glassblowers used their artistic talents and traditional molds to create many wonderful shapes and designs exclusively to appeal to the American family during this time of great national pride. In 1926, the Liberty Bell ornament was designed to commemorate the 150th anniversary of the Declaration of Independence. Delicately molded into the side of the ornament is the inscription "1776-1926", representing one hundred and fifty years of freedom.

Flags are a national symbol of freedom and pride. The flag of the United States of America is one of the oldest national standards in the world; older than the Union Jack of Great Britain and the Tricolor of France. The colors in "Old Glory" and their arrangement are often seen as expressing the very character of the nation. George Washington described the white in the flag as symbolizing Americans' desire for liberty. The red signified the courage and sacrifices of the nation's defenders, and the blue has been likened to the loyalty and unity of its citizens. The Flag on Ball ornament thus pays tribute to American patriotism.

Old World Christmas®

Admiral **Robert Peary** of the United States Navy is credited as the first man to lead an expedition to the North Pole. After twenty-three years of exploration and preparation for the trek, his party finally reached their destination on April 6, 1909. An extremely romantic but lonely man, Peary reached his life-long goal in a dog sled named 'The Josephine' in memory of his wife, and claimed the Pole in honor of the United States with an American flag which she had sewn by hand. Admiral Peary's devotion, perseverance and courage are an inspiration to all who dream of great achievements. The Admiral Peary glass ornament serves as a reminder of all we can accomplish through strength and dedication.

Apples were the traditional Christian symbol of temptation. Apple ornaments were hung on evergreen trees during the presentation of the Paradise plays of the Christmas season in medieval times throughout Europe. Trees laden with apple ornaments were used during the reenactment of the story of Adam and Eve on Christmas Eve, to reinforce the meaning of Christ's birth. Also, an early legend held that if an apple was cut during the holidays and there was a perfect star inside and the seeds were plump, good health and fortune would be assured during the coming year. As the earliest Christmas trees were adorned with natural fruits and nuts, glassblowers naturally patterned many of their first molds after these items.

Carrots have long held a special place in German legend. The glass Carrot ornament is truly a decoration that can bring a tear to an old woman's eye. Long ago the glass Carrot ornament was very popular in Germany as a traditional gift for brides. It was believed to bring the bride good luck in the kitchen. After being lost for many years, the antique mold has resurfaced and German artisans are again creating this treasure for a bride's first Christmas tree.

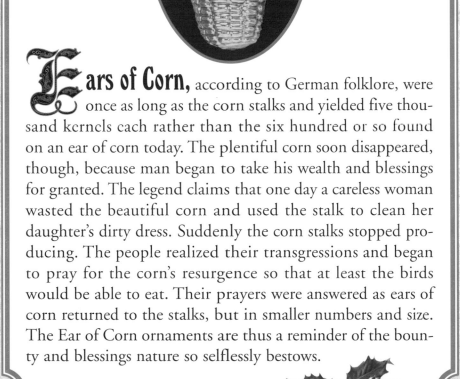

Ears of Corn, according to German folklore, were once as long as the corn stalks and yielded five thousand kernels each rather than the six hundred or so found on an ear of corn today. The plentiful corn soon disappeared, though, because man began to take his wealth and blessings for granted. The legend claims that one day a careless woman wasted the beautiful corn and used the stalk to clean her daughter's dirty dress. Suddenly the corn stalks stopped producing. The people realized their transgressions and began to pray for the corn's resurgence so that at least the birds would be able to eat. Their prayers were answered as ears of corn returned to the stalks, but in smaller numbers and size. The Ear of Corn ornaments are thus a reminder of the bounty and blessings nature so selflessly bestows.

Oranges have always been considered a very special treat at Christmas time. Costly and scarce during the winter months many years ago, oranges were highly appreciated and were quite a delicacy. Santa would often leave one of these sweet fruits in the toe of the stocking of good little girls or boys as a delightful reward. Oranges were among the first figural glass ornaments produced, reflecting the adornments of the earliest Christmas trees in their natural splendor.

Tomatoes, long considered "love apples," were originally thought to be unpalatable and poisonous by some cultures. Even so, the tomato's popularity flourished because gardeners prized it as a fast-growing legume that would rapidly cover arbors, outbuildings, and privies. In the 1840's the Germans declared the tomato suitable to eat. With the tomato's red and green Christmas colors, it seemed only natural that the early mold makers would create a mold for this festive vegetable.

Grape ornaments were symbols of friendship. Not only was the giving of a grape ornament a German pledge of friendship, it was also symbolic of sharing a friendly glass of wine. The German countryside was dotted with vineyards nestled among steep hillsides. Young men carefully made their way along curving little cobblestone paths in search of succulent vine-ripened grapes. The grapes were later shared with friends in the form of a perfectly-aged bottle of Riesling or other German vintage.

Old World Christmas®

Pickle ornaments were considered a special decoration by many families in Germany where the fir tree was decorated on Christmas Eve. The pickle was always the last ornament to be hung on the Christmas tree, with the parents hiding it in the green boughs among the other ornaments. When the children were allowed to view the tree for the first time, they would begin gleefully searching for the Pickle ornament. The children knew that whoever first found that special ornament would receive an extra little gift left by St. Nicholas for being the most observant child.

Acorns have long been thought to be good luck symbols in Germany where oak trees are considered sacred. The German saying "from little acorns come mighty oaks" depicts the protective nature of a mother's belief that when one provides nurturing and care, one can anticipate great results. Acorns are also believed by the German people to represent the rebirth of life as witnessed through the coming of the Christ child. Early German Christmas trees were laden with cones, cookies and nuts, most notably the acorn, to commemorate this gift of life and luck. This tradition is still celebrated today with the glass Acorn ornament.

ones were natural decorations that grew on majestic fir and pine trees, so they were naturally among the first molded glass ornaments produced. Cones were believed to be symbols of motherhood and fertility. An old legend surrounding cones offered additional symbolism: "One winter's day, a poor old woman and her family went out to gather cones on the mountainside to use for fuel. Suddenly an obliging little elf appeared from under an evergreen tree and directed them to where the best cones could be found. As the baskets were filled, they grew increasingly heavy, until the old woman and her children could hardly carry them. But suddenly to their delight, their burdens lightened when they discovered that every cone they had selected had magically turned into silver!"

Fir Trees are one of the most widely recognized symbols of the holiday season. The role of the fir tree in mid-winter celebrations dates back to pre-Christian times when the tree symbolized nature's triumph over winter's darkness and deathly cold. Christians began using fir trees and other evergreens as a reminder of Christ's gift of everlasting life. The fir tree was also popular because of its paternal nature. Thick fir tree boughs graciously protected delicate birds, and provided shelter to other animals in the dense Bavarian forests of Germany.

Old World Christmas®

Holly, with its red berries, dark glossy green leaves, and thorny tips was a symbol of life in the bleak chill of winter. The bright colors of the holly made it a natural symbol of rebirth and life in the winter whiteness of northern Europe. The appearance of the flaming red holly berries opened the season of feasting and good cheer. Also, in late December, German villagers would traditionally place holly around the interior of their dwellings to ward off bad winter weather and unwanted spirits. In early years, Father Christmas often decorated his hood with holly, which represented the crown of thorns that Jesus wore when he was crucified, and the red berries were symbolic of the blood he shed. The Holly Heart ornament is decorated with colorful sprigs of this beloved Christmas greenery.

Ornament Legends

Pansies are considered to be sentimental flowers, as they have been since Victorian times, symbolizing thoughts and feelings of love. It is believed that Cupid shot an arrow into a pansy, which turned the blossom's pure white to purple and gave the flower great power. Through the ages, pansies have also been called "heartsease," for their heart-shaped leaves were said to cure a broken heart.

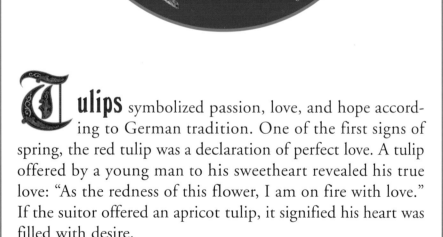

Tulips symbolized passion, love, and hope according-
ing to German tradition. One of the first signs of
spring, the red tulip was a declaration of perfect love. A tulip
offered by a young man to his sweetheart revealed his true
love: "As the redness of this flower, I am on fire with love."
If the suitor offered an apricot tulip, it signified his heart was
filled with desire.

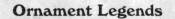

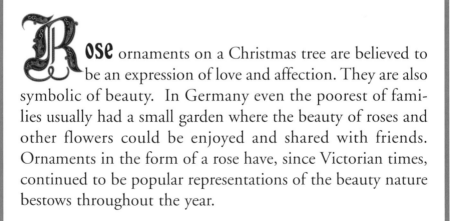

Rose ornaments on a Christmas tree are believed to be an expression of love and affection. They are also symbolic of beauty. In Germany even the poorest of families usually had a small garden where the beauty of roses and other flowers could be enjoyed and shared with friends. Ornaments in the form of a rose have, since Victorian times, continued to be popular representations of the beauty nature bestows throughout the year.

Rosen Cavalier, also known as the Knight of the Rose, was created to commemorate Der Rosenkavalier Opera, a romantic comedy portraying Viennese life in the mid-eighteenth century, written by Richard Strauss in 1911. A popular and frequently performed German opera, Der Rosenkavalier's enduring appeal is due to its profusion of memorable melodies and famous waltzes. This, combined with the Rosen Cavalier's traditional role as a deliverer of proposals of marriage, made this figure a unique and touching gift for engagements, weddings, and anniversaries. Lost for more than eighty years, the Rosen Cavalier ornament mold was recently located and made available for today's sentimental suitors.

St. Nicholas, according to ancient legend, was known to be a kind, benevolent man and was legendary for performing miracles. St. Nicholas was charitable, always ready to help the needy, and later became the patron saint of children.

St. Nicholas was the European equivalent of the American Santa Claus. He was a thin figure, clothed in bishop's robes, who rode into town on a white horse on

St. Nicholas's Day, December 6. The holiday season began on this day in Europe, and St. Nicholas' Eve was a night to which children everywhere looked forward with eager anticipation. On this widely-celebrated holiday, parents instructed their children to leave their shoes by the door in hopes that St. Nicholas would fill them with treats. Good boys and girls often received fruit, nuts and candy, but bad boys and girls found nothing but a rod, switch or lump of coal.

It is thought that the giving of gifts to small children during the holidays originated directly from the legend of their patron saint, St. Nicholas. Holiday gift giving was first observed in France during the Middle Ages, when nuns would leave charitable gifts for the poor and needy on the eve of St. Nicholas' Day, in his honor. The practice of bestowing gifts on children on December 6 quickly spread throughout Europe, and the night of December 5 was often celebrated with parades, festivities and merriment of all kinds.

Today, families in Europe continue to commence the celebration of the Christmas holidays on St. Nicholas's Eve, December 5, and often attend a midnight mass. The legend of St. Nicholas and his kind generosity has endured to this day, and the benevolence he represents is a permanent part of the magic of the holidays.

Cornucopia of Toys ornaments bring to life the joy of Christmas through the eyes of a child. On their first day of school, German children leave home tightly clutching a paper cone full of surprises. This cone-shaped container, called a schultüte in German, was lovingly assembled by the child's parents. It was filled with sweets and miniature toys and was meant to diminish any anxiety the youngster might experience while away from home for the first time. The Cornucopia of Toys ornament represents this comforting gift from parent to child.

anta Claus truly represents a veritable melting pot of cultures, beliefs and traditions. As immigrants arrived in the New World centuries ago, along with their hopes and dreams for a better future, they brought with them their beliefs and customs surrounding the holidays. The Germans brought their Belsnickel and Christkindl, the Scandinavians their gift-giving elves and the Dutch introduced their Sinterklaas, all representing the celebration of St. Nicholas.

The American legend of Santa Claus embodies childhood innocence and magical delight, as Santa Claus is the bearer of gifts and treats for children everywhere. With his home at the wintry North Pole, he and his merry elves created the toys that put the magic into the holidays. He was a kind and gentle figure, and starry-eyed children awaited his annual visit with spirited anticipation. On Christmas Eve, the eve of the birth of the Christ child, Santa Claus magically flew around the world in his sleigh, filled with toys and gifts and drawn by eight reindeer. Parents had their children hang their stockings by the fire, in hopes that Santa Claus would come. He stopped at each child's home and slid down the chimney to leave special packages and surprises in their stockings. Wide-eyed good girls and boys would discover wonderful gifts in their stockings, but bad boys and girls would only find a lump of coal.

The legend of Santa Claus is derived in part from the benevolent European figure St. Nicholas, and in part from American writers who wrote children's poems in the nineteenth century. Clement Moore, who wrote "A Visit From St. Nicholas" in 1822, and Thomas Nast, the famed political cartoonist who depicted Santa Claus in the 1860's as an elfin figure, contributed greatly to this fantasy. Their descriptions of the jolly man clad in red and white created the folk hero children around the world dream about on Christmas Eve. This American patron saint of children certainly brings joy and delight to all during the holidays.

ℳrs. Santa Claus was originally created simply

because the German glassblowers felt that she would be appealing to the American public. Since Santa Claus evolved from St. Nicholas, a celibate priest, there was no demand for a Mrs. Claus ornament in Germany. Very few early Mrs. Claus ornaments were made because some considered it sacrilegious to bestow a wife upon a priest. In time, the family concept took hold as German families began to secularize Christmas and Mrs. Claus was fondly welcomed to the celebration.

Old World Christmas®

Stockings were relatively late additions to the Christmas celebration. The oldest reference to the Christmas stocking appeared in 1821, in the children's book "A New Year's Present," published in New York. It is often forgotten that today's Christmas stocking originally was a gift-bearing rival to the Christmas tree. In fact, the stocking versus the tree debate continued into the first part of the twentieth century when most families began to happily embrace both customs. This delightful ornament features a Victorian stocking overflowing with toys following a visit from Santa Claus. A cute teddy bear awaits its delighted new friend.

Humpty Dumpty is a well-known and often quoted nursery rhyme that was written in the fifteenth century when King Richard III ruled England. Just as Humpty Dumpty sat on a wall and had a great fall, King Richard III quickly ascended the throne and then suddenly fell from power. Richard's fall was great and no amount of effort from his few supporters would return him to the throne.

Hey Diddle Diddle, the cat and the fiddle... is both a child-pleasing nursery rhyme and a political jest at England's Queen Elizabeth I, who was known for her delight in laughter and merrymaking. Elizabeth was nick-named "the cat" by her subjects because she toyed with her cabinet members like a cat playing with mice. Remembered for her love of music, Elizabeth was often rumored to "let down her crown" and dance in her chambers to the festive sounds of the fiddle.

Nutcrackers were traditionally dressed as soldiers and kings. In old Germany, it delighted villagers to see these authoritarian figures doing menial tasks such as cracking nuts! A bowl of Christmas nuts was just not complete without a colorful German nutcracker standing at attention nearby. Nutcrackers were especially popular with Germans who coined the phrase, "Gott gibt die Nüsse aber knacken müss man sie selbst (God gives the nuts but we have to crack them ourselves)," which was intended to teach children that life was hard but rewarding. This phrase made the nutcracker a favorite toy, possibly because it enabled children to reach life's rewards more easily.

Walnuts were frequently part of early Christmas celebrations in Europe that included evenings of games and merrymaking. Tiny candles, stuck in walnut shells, were set afloat in a pan of water. The little boy's candle which burned to the end without capsizing was promised a long life, and the girl's candle which stood upright the longest would have the best husband. During such celebrations parents would crack walnuts trusting the nut would not be spoiled; if it was, death was foretold to that person. These simple traditions were memorialized through the years by the walnut ornament. The ornament also recalled the earliest of all ornaments, the brightly painted walnuts that adorned the first Christmas trees.

Old World Christmas®

Merlin was best known as the wise advisor and court magician to the mythical King Arthur. He was also closely linked with nature and gained his magical strength from the forests. As King Arthur's advisor, Merlin used his powers and wisdom to help Arthur obtain Excalibur from the Lady of the Lake. Merlin and the Arthurian legends also appealed to a sense of justice and romance where heroes abounded and good dominated over evil. These values were especially appropriate at Christmas time and remain an integral part of the holiday spirit.

John Bull was to English citizens what Uncle Sam was to citizens of the United States. In the 1700's John Bull appeared as a jolly, honest, plain-dealing, hot-tempered farmer. Gradually, in the 1800's, he was transformed into a refined, respectable English gentleman. It was this later image that was portrayed by the John Bull ornament to remind one of the admirable qualities of citizenship and civic pride.

Old World Christmas®

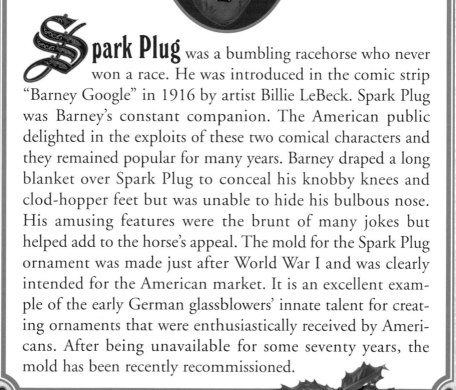

Spark Plug was a bumbling racehorse who never won a race. He was introduced in the comic strip "Barney Google" in 1916 by artist Billie LeBeck. Spark Plug was Barney's constant companion. The American public delighted in the exploits of these two comical characters and they remained popular for many years. Barney draped a long blanket over Spark Plug to conceal his knobby knees and clod-hopper feet but was unable to hide his bulbous nose. His amusing features were the brunt of many jokes but helped add to the horse's appeal. The mold for the Spark Plug ornament was made just after World War I and was clearly intended for the American market. It is an excellent example of the early German glassblowers' innate talent for creating ornaments that were enthusiastically received by Americans. After being unavailable for some seventy years, the mold has been recently recommissioned.

Ornament Legends

Zeppelins were grand airships created in the mid-nineteenth century. The Commemorative Zeppelin ornament portrayed the rigid structure airship, "Graf Zeppelin", invented by Count Ferdinand Von Zeppelin, 1838-1917. The figures on this zeppelin ornament are Count Zeppelin and Hugo Eckener, who was the first captain of the Graf Zeppelin. The zeppelin was an early twentieth-century phenomenon that provided a form of passenger air travel that fascinated the world. It was also used by the military, and greatly appealed to Americans who were intrigued with these new flying machines and the possibilities of trans-Atlantic transportation.

About the Authors...

Tim and Beth Merck

Many years ago, Tim and Beth Merck owned a retail store in Spokane, Washington, in which they sold antiques imported directly from Europe. In 1975, during an antiques buying trip Tim and Beth made to Germany, they purchased a large assortment of German Christmas decorations to sell in America. This new venture proved to be remarkably successful and they had difficulty meeting the demands of collectors and dealers for these new-found treasures. They are now the proud owners of Old World Christmas, a major importer of authentic German collectibles, best known for its genuine figural glass German Christmas ornaments with the star cap. Today, Beth has become the critically acclaimed artist known to collectors throughout the world as E.M. Merck.

Inspired by the heirloom figural glass decorations Beth's grandmother had on her tree, Tim and Beth traveled to all parts of Germany in search of these precious ornaments. Driving from village to village, and literally knocking on door after door in search of suppliers, Tim and Beth befriended many storytellers along the way who were eager to share bits of their heritage. Their twenty years of extensive travels and close associations with the artisans who create the authentic quality ornaments with the star cap have provided them with a wealth of knowledge. Tim, with his degree in European History from the University of Idaho, and Beth, who studied Fine Arts, Art History, and German cultural traditions at Pomona College, Gonzaga and Eastern Washington Universities and graduated with a degree in Fine Arts, were enthralled as they learned firsthand about the age-old traditions of the German people through family gatherings, business associations, holiday festivals and evenings sipping beer in quaint village pubs.

It is little wonder to Tim and Beth Merck that the richness and charm of these Christmas legends originated in the small glassblower villages nestled deep in the mountainous forests in the heart of Germany. It is here that these traditions are preserved in the form of glass ornaments still mouth-blown in the same antique molds used by their ancestors. These peoples' appreciation of life and nature, combined with a genuine enjoyment of the heritage of their fables and legends, has provided Tim and Beth with an abundance of magical stories, which they now share in the hope of enriching Christmas celebrations for us all. They take great pleasure in presenting these cherished tales of German traditions to you and your family.

Old World Christmas Legend Index

The following is a listing of Old World Christmas ornaments featured with the legends within this book. There are many additional ornaments within the Old World Christmas collection which also represent these legends. Contact your favorite retailer for additional information.

Listed by legend, page number, item number, and the name of the ornament(s) pictured with the legend.

Old World Christmas®

RABBIT - Page 15
 1201   Hungry Rabbit

RED RIDING HOOD - Page 23
 1053   Red Riding Hood

ROSE - Page 54
 3628   Clip-On Pink Rose

ROSEN CAVALIER - Page 55
 2490   Rosen Cavalier

ST. NICHOLAS - Page 57
 4081   Regal Father Christmas

SANTA CLAUS - Page 61
 4076   Very Merry Santa

SPARK PLUG - Page 73
 1292   Spark Plug

STAR - Page 27
 2205   Shining Star

STOCKING - Page 65
 4410   Stocking with Toys

TOMATO - Page 42
 2858   Large Tomato

TULIP - Page 53
 3673   Assorted Red Tulips

WALNUT - Page 70
 2804   Large Walnut

WEATHER FROG - Page 17
 1233   Weather Frog

ZEPPELIN - Page 75
 4607   Commemorative
          Airship

Join the Club!

Membership in the Old World Christmas Collectors' Club is available through the following address. Annual dues are $30.00.
Members are entitled to free gifts, newsletters, the Collectors' Guide and special offerings of limited-edition collectors' pieces, only available to Club members.

Old World Christmas Collectors' Club™
P.O. Box 8000 • Dept. C • Spokane, WA 99203
Phone: 1-800-962-7669

Old World Christmas®

Acknowledgements

*We sincerely appreciate those who inspired
and contributed to this book.*

Fran Frané
Dolores and Mel Merck
Robert Merck
James Morrison
Debra Mosier
The Müller-Blech Family
and
the many individuals
who shared the stories
of their family Christmases.